CONTENTS

KT-481-330

GETTING STARTED

200 million people all over the world speak French. Why not join them?

In this book, you will learn many essential words and phrases. These will help you to communicate in all kinds of everyday situations, from making friends, to shopping for clothes, or finding your way round!

Each French word comes with its English translation and an indication of how to pronounce it.

un ordinateur . . . . .French word
urn or-dee-nat-ur . . . .*rough pronunciation*
a computer . . . . .English translation

For more tips on how to pronounce French words, check out the pronunciation guide on page 32.

Here are just some of the countries where French is spoken:

la France
la fraunss
France

l'Algérie
lal-shay-ree
Algeria

les Antilles
lez aun-tee
The West Indies

le Canada
lur ka-na-da
Canada

le Maroc
lur ma-rok
Morocco

la Polynésie
la po-lee-nay-zee
Polynesia

la Belgique
la bel-sheek
Belgium

la Tunisie
la too-nee-zee
Tunisia

la Suisse
la sweess
Switzerland

le Sénégal
lur say-nay-gal
Senegal

EVERYDAY FRENCH

by Sue Finnie and Danièle Bourdais

C153648696

KENT
LIBRARIES & ARCHIVES

C153648696

Copyright © **ticktock Entertainment Ltd** 2008
First published in Great Britain in 2008 by **ticktock Media Ltd**,
2 Orchard Business Centre, North Farm Road, Tunbridge Wells, Kent, TN2 3XF

written by Sue Finnie and Danièle Bourdais
French translation by Danièle Bourdais
ticktock project editor: Joe Harris
ticktock project designer: Simon Fenn
ticktock picture researcher: Lizzie Knowles
French language consultant: Sara McKenna

ISBN-13: 978 1 84696 784 9 pbk

Printed in China

A CIP catalogue record for this book is available from the British Library.

No part of this publication may be reproduced, copied, stored in a retrieval system or transmitted in any
form or by any means electronic, mechanical, photocopying, recording or otherwise without prior written
permission of the copyright owner.

Picture credits (t=top; b=bottom; c=centre; l=left; r=right):
age fotostock/ SuperStock: 25t. BananaStock/ SuperStock: 10tr, 11tc, 16tl, 16tr, 21tl, OBCt. Corbis/
SuperStock: 10tl. Creatas/ SuperStock: 23tl. ImageSource/ SuperStock: 8tr, 12t. iStock: 1, 5b, 6tc,
7bl, 8bl, 9tl, 11c x2, 13t (sister), 13c (uncle), 13b (snake), 15tr, 15cr, 15bl, 15fbc, 16cr, 16bl, 19tc,
19tr, 20tl, 20c (coffee), 20bl (hotel), 22c (dress), 24cr, 27tl, 27tr, 28tl, 28cl, 29tl, 29cl, 29cc, 29bl,
29bc, 30tl, 30cl, 30cr, 31tl, 31tc, 31cr, 31bc x2. Jupiter Images: OFC, 12b, 14b, 18tl, 26tl, 29br.
Photo alto/ SuperStock: 31cr. Photodisc/ SuperStock: 7br. Photolibrary Group: 26tr. Purestock/
SuperStock: 7tr, 24tl. Shutterstock: 2, 4 all, 5c, 6tl, 6tr x2, 6b all, 7tl, 7tc, 7c all, 8b (clocks), 9b all, 10b
all, 11tl, 11tr, 11cl, 11cr, 11b all, 12c, 13 all, 14t, 14cl, 14cr, 15tl, 15tc x2, 15cl, 15cc x2, 15bc x2,
15br, 15fbl, 15fbc, 15fbr, 16cl, 16br, 17 all, 18tr, 18c all, 18b all, 19b all, 20tr, 20b all, 21tr, 21b all,
22 all, 23tr, 23b all, 24tr, 24cl, 24c, 24b all, 25cl, 25cr, 25b all, 26b all, 27bl, 27br, 28tc, 28tr, 28cc,
28bl, 28bc x2, 28br, 29tc, 29tr, 29cr, 30tc, 30tr, 30cc, 30bl, 31tr, 31cc, 31bl, 31br x2, 32cr, OBCb.
ticktock Media archive: 5t. Neil Tingle/ actionplus: 19tl. David Young-Wolff/ Alamy: 8tl.

Every effort has been made to trace copyright holders, and we apologise in advance for any omissions.
We would be pleased to insert the appropriate acknowledgments in any subsequent
edition of this publication.

FRANCE FACTS

- France is more than twice as big as the UK.

- 61 million people live in France.

- The French flag is blue, white and red.

- The capital of France is Paris.

- French money is the euro.

- The highest mountain in Europe, Mont Blanc, is in France.

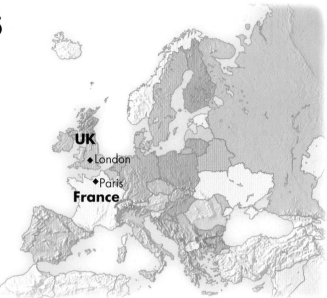

UK
♦London
♦Paris
France

KEY WORDS

Peut-être.
Pur-tet-tr.
Maybe.

Oui.
Wee.
Yes.

Je ne sais pas.
Sh nur say pa.
I don't know.

Bien sûr!
Bee-an soor!
Of course!

Non.
Non.
No.

Pardon.
Par-don.
Sorry.

HELP!

If you don't understand what a French person is saying to you, here are some useful phrases:

Je ne comprends pas.
Sh nur kom-praun pa.
I don't understand.

Parlez-vous anglais?
Par-lay-voo aun-glay?
Do you speak English?

Répétez, s'il vous plaît.
Ray-pay-tay, seel voo play.
Could you repeat that, please.

Comment-dit on...?
Ko-maun deet-on?
How do you say...?

Sometimes the French word that you use will depend on whether you are male or female.

This symbol (♀) shows that a word describes a woman or girl.

This (♂) shows that a word describes a man or boy.

MAKING NEW FRIENDS

Tu t'appelles comment?
Too tap-el kom-aun?
What's your name?

Je m'appelle Anna.
Sh map-el a-na.
My name's Anna.

Bonjour!	Salut!
Bon-shoor!	*Sa-loo!*
Hello!	Hi!

Tu parles quelles langues?
Too parl kel laung?
What languages do you speak?

Je parle anglais et français.
Sh parl aun-glay ay fraun-say.
I speak English and French.

Tu viens d'où?
Too vee-an doo?
Where are you from?

Je viens de
Grande-Bretagne.
Sh vee-an dur graund-brur-tann-yuh.
I'm from Britain.

l'Espagne
less-pan-yuh
Spain

la France
la fraunss
France

l'Italie
lee-ta-lee
Italy

l'Allemagne
lal-man-yuh
Germany

la Pologne
la po-lon-yuh
Poland

la Chine
la sheen
China

J'ai un petit copain♂/
une petite copine.♀
*Shay urn pur-tee kop-an/
oon pur-teet ko-peen.*
I have a boyfriend/a
girlfriend.

Tu me donnes ton
numéro de portable?
*Too mur don ton
noo-may-ro dur por-ta-bl?*
Can you give me your
mobile number?

Tu veux danser avec moi?
Too vur daun-say av-ek mwa?
Do you want to dance with me?

Qu'est-ce que tu aimes?
Kes-ka too aym?
What are you into?

la mode
la mod
fashion

la danse
la daunss
dancing

le sport
lur spor
sport

les films
lay feelm
films

les jeux vidéo
lay shur vee-day-o
video games

Tu me donnes ton adresse
email?
Too mur don ton a-dress ee-mel?
Can you give me your
email address?

Mon email, c'est...
Mon ee-mel, say...
My email is...

Au revoir!
O rev-war!
Good bye!

A bientôt!
A bee-an-to!
See you soon!

IT'S A DATE

Tu as quel âge?
Too a kel ash?
How old are you?

J'ai seize ans.
Shay sez aun.
I'm sixteen years old.

C'est quand, ton anniversaire?
Say kaun, ton nan-ee-vair-sair?
When's your birthday?

Mon anniversaire, c'est le onze mai.
Mon nan-ee-vair-sair, say lur onz may.
My birthday's on the 11th of May.

Combien?
Kom-bee-an?
How many?

1	**2**	**3**	**4**	**5**	**6**	**7**	**8**	**9**	**10**	**11**
un	deux	trois	quatre	cinq	six	sept	huit	neuf	dix	onze
urn	*dur*	*trwa*	*kat-r*	*sank*	*seess*	*set*	*weet*	*nurf*	*deess*	*onz*
one	two	three	four	five	six	seven	eight	nine	ten	eleven

12	**13**	**14**	**15**	**16**	**17**	**18**	**19**	**20**
douze	treize	quatorze	quinze	seize	dix-sept	dix-huit	dix-neuf	vingt
dooz	*trez*	*kat-orz*	*kanz*	*sez*	*dee-set*	*dee-zweet*	*deez-nurf*	*van*
twelve	thirteen	fourteen	fifteen	sixteen	seventeen	eighteen	nineteen	twenty

Quelle heure est-il?
Kel ur ett-eel?
What's the time?

six heures et quart
seez ur ay kar
quarter past six

quatre heures dix
katr ur deess
ten past four

dix heures et demie
deez ur ay dem-ee
half past ten

deux heures moins vingt
durz ur mwan van
twenty to two

midi moins le quart
mee-dee mwan lur kar
quarter to twelve

une heure
oon ur
one o'clock

Les jours de la semaine
Lay joor dur la sur-men
Days of the week

A sept heures, vendredi soir!
A set ur, vaun-dr-dee swar!
See you at seven o'clock on
Friday evening!

mardi
mar-dee
Tuesday

mercredi
mer-kr-dee
Wednesday

lundi
lurn-dee
Monday

jeudi
shur-dee
Thursday

dimanche
dee-maunsh
Sunday

vendredi
vaun-dr-dee
Friday

samedi
sam-dee
Saturday

L'année
La-nay
The year

l'été
lay-tay
summer

juin
shoo-an
June

juillet
shwee-yay
July

août
oot
August

Halloween
al-o-ween
Halloween

mai
may
May

l'automne
lo-ton
autumn

Pâques
pak
Easter

avril
av-reel
April

septembre
sep-taun-br
September

mars
marss
March

octobre
okt-o-br
October

le printemps
lur pran-taun
spring

novembre
no-vaun-br
November

février
fay-vree-yay
February

l'hiver
lee-vair
winter

janvier
shaun-vee-yay
January

décembre
day-saun-br
December

la Saint-Valentin
la san val-aun-tan
Valentine's Day

Noël
no-el
Christmas

SNACK ATTACK!

Vous désirez?
Voo dayz-ee-ray?
What would you like?

Mon repas préféré, c'est un hamburger
et un milk-shake.
*Mon re-pa pray-fay-ray, set urn am-bur-gur
ay urn meelk-shayk.*
My favourite meal is hamburger and milkshake.

Le menu
Lur mur-noo
Menu

du poulet
doo poo-lay
chicken

des pâtes
day pat
pasta

du pain
doo pan
bread

du jambon
doo jaun-bon
ham

un sandwich
urn saun-dweetsh
a sandwich

des légumes verts
day lay-goom vair
green vegetables

des frites
day freet
chips

une salade mixte
oon sa-lad mixt
a mixed salad

une pizza
oon pee-dza
a pizza

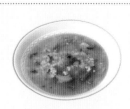

une soupe
oon soop
soup

Je bois du lait le matin.
Sh bwa doo lay lur mat-an.
I drink milk in the morning.

Je mange de la salade
tous les jours.
*Sh maunsh dur la sa-lad
too lay shoor.*
I eat salad every day.

Je déteste les fruits!
Sh day-test lay froo-ee!
I hate fruit!

Les boissons
Lay bwa-son
Drinks

un jus d'orange
urn joo do-raun-sh
an orange juice

un verre d'eau
urn vair do
a glass of water

un chocolat chaud
urn sho-ko-la sho
a hot chocolate

un soda
urn so-da
a fizzy drink

Les glaces
Lay glass
Ice cream

Vous avez quels parfums?
Voo za-vay kel parf-an?
What flavours have you got?

café
kaf-fay
coffee

vanille
va-nee
vanilla

fraise
frez
strawberry

chocolat
sho-ko-la
chocolate

citron
see-tron
lemon

menthe
maunt
mint

WHO'S WHO?

1 Elle a les cheveux blonds.
El a lay shur-vur blon.
She's got blonde hair.

2 les oreilles percées
lay zor-ay-ee pair-say
pierced ears

3 les cheveux longs
lay shur-vur lon
long hair

4 les yeux bleus
lay zyur blur
blue eyes

5 les cheveux raides
lay shur-vur red
straight hair

6 des lunettes
day loo-net
glasses

7 une frange
oon fraun-sh
a fringe

8 la bouche
la boosh
mouth

9 les dents
lay daun
teeth

10 un appareil dentaire
urn ap-a-ray-ee daun-tair
braces`

11 le nez
le nay
nose

12 Il a les cheveux noirs.
Eel a lay shur-vur nwar.
He's got black hair.

13 les cheveux courts
lay shur-vur koor
short hair

14 les yeux marron
lay zyur ma-ron
brown eyes

15 la joue
la shoo
cheek

16 le menton
lur maun-ton
chin

17 le cou
lur koo
neck

Voici ma famille.
Vwa-see ma fam-ee.
Here's my family.

Tu as des frères et sœurs?
Too a day frair ay sur?
Have you got any brothers and sisters?

J'ai deux frères et une sœur.
Shay dur frair ay oon sur.
I've got two brothers and a sister.

mon père
mon pair
my dad

ma mère
ma mair
my mum

mon frère
mon frair
my brother

ma sœur
ma sur
my sister

moi
mwa
me

ma grand-mère
ma graun-mair
my grandmother

mon grand-père
mon graun-pair
my grandfather

mon cousin
mon koo-zan
my cousin

ma tante
ma taunt
my aunt

mon oncle
mon onkl
my uncle

Les animaux domestiques
Lay zan-ee-mo dom-ess-teek
Pets

Tu as des animaux?
Too a day zan-ee-mo?
Have you got any pets?

une souris
oon soo-ree
a mouse

un hamster
urn am-stair
a hamster

une perruche
oon pair-oosh
a budgie

J'ai un chien.
Shay urn shee-an.
I've got a dog.

un chat
urn sha
a cat

un poisson rouge
urn pwa-son roosh
a goldfish

un lapin
urn la-pan
a rabbit

un serpent
urn sair-paun
a snake

DRESS TO IMPRESS

Les vêtements que je préfère, c'est les jeans et les t-shirts.
Lay vet-maun ke sh pray-fayr, say lay jean ay lay tee-shurt.
My favourite clothes are jeans and t-shirts.

Je peux essayer?
Sh pur ay-say-yay?
Can I try this on?

Ça me va?
Sa mur va?
Does it suit me?

Oui, ça fait super!
Wee, sa fay soo-per!
Yes, it looks great!

Je porte des baskets le week-end.
Sh port day ba-sket lur week-end.
I wear trainers at the weekend.

bleu	vert	jaune	orange	rouge	rose	violet	noir	blanc
blur	*vair*	*shon*	*o-raun-sh*	*roosh*	*roz*	*vee-o-lay*	*nwaar*	*blaun*
blue	green	yellow	orange	red	pink	purple	black	white

des boucles d'oreilles
day boo-kl do-ray-ee
earrings

une jupe
oon shoop
a skirt

une casquette
oon kas-ket
a cap

un haut à capuche
urn o a ka-poosh
a hooded top

une écharpe
oon ay-sharp
a scarf

des lunettes de soleil
day loo-net dur so-lay-ee
sunglasses

une veste
oon vest
a jacket

des gants
day gaun
gloves

une robe
oon rob
a dress

un sac
urn sak
a bag

une ceinture
oon san-toor
a belt

un short
urn short
shorts

des sandales
day saun-dal
sandals

un pull
urn pool
a pullover

un pantalon
urn paun-ta-lon
trousers

des chaussures
day sho-soor
shoes

HI-TECH

Je vais envoyer un SMS.
Sh vay aun-vwa-yay urn ess-em-ess.
I'll send a text message.

Je discute avec mes amis sur Internet.
Sh dee-skoot av-ek may zam-ee soor an-tair-net.
I chat with my friends on the Internet.

On prend une photo?
On praun oon fo-to?
Shall we take a photo?

J'ai besoin de vérifier mes emails.
Shay bur-zwan dur vay-rif-ee-yay may zee-mel.
I need to check my emails.

N'oublie pas de recharger ton portable!
Noo-blee pa dur re-shar-shay ton por-ta-bl!
Don't forget to charge your mobile!

On adore les jeux vidéo.
On nad-or lay shur vee-day-o.
We love video games.

la radio
la rad-yo
radio

un caméscope
urn kam-ay-skop
a camcorder

un ordinateur portable
urn or-dee-nat-ur por-ta-bl
a laptop

Un ordinateur
Urn or-dee-nat-ur
A computer

l'écran
lay-kraun
computer screen

la webcam
la web-kam
webcam

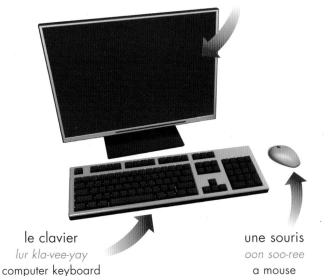

le clavier
lur kla-vee-yay
computer keyboard

une souris
oon soo-ree
a mouse

un appareil photo
urn ap-ar-ay-ee fo-to
a camera

une console de jeux
oon kon-sol dur shur
a games console

un lecteur DVD
urn lek-tur day-vay-day
a DVD player

un lecteur MP3
urn lek-tur em-pay-trwa
an iPod/MP3 player

un (téléphone) portable
urn (tay-lay-fon) por-ta-bl
a mobile phone

un DVD
urn day-vay-day
a DVD

la télévision
la tay-lay-viz-yon
television

FREE TIME

Je joue dans un groupe.
Sh shoo dan zurn groop.
I play in a band.

J'aime le hip-hop. *Shem lur eep-op.* I like hip-hop.	la dance *la daunss* dance	le rock *lur rock* rock
le métal *lur may-al* heavy metal	le R 'n' B *lur ar-en-bee* R 'n' B	la pop *la pop* pop

Tu joues d'un instrument?
Too shoo durn an-stroo-maun?
Do you play an instrument?

le clavier électronique
lur klav-yay el-ek-tro-neek
keyboard

le piano
lur pee-an-o
piano

le violon
lur vee-o-lon
violin

la batterie
la bat-ree
drums

la guitare électrique
la gee-tar el-ek-treek
electric guitar

le saxophone
lur sax-o-fon
saxophone

la flûte
la floot
flute

Tu supportes quelle
équipe de foot?
*Too soo-port kel
ay-keep dur foot?*
Which football team do
you support?

On a perdu 1 à 0.
On na per-doo urn a zay-ro.
We lost the match 1–0.

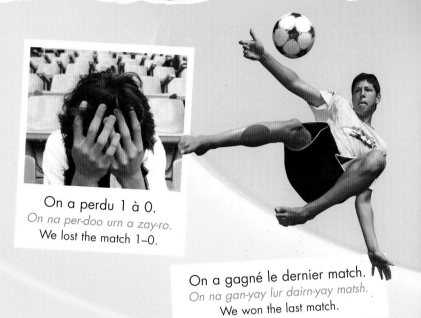

On a gagné le dernier match.
On na gan-yay lur dairn-yay matsh.
We won the last match.

Quel sport est-ce que tu aimes?
Kel spor ess-ka too em?
What sport do you like?

le rugby
lur roog-bee
rugby

le tennis
lur tay-neess
tennis

l'équitation
lay-kee-tass-yon
horse-riding

la natation
la nat-ass-yon
swimming

le vélo
lur vay-lo
cycling

l'athlétisme
lat-lay-tee-sm
running

le judo
lur shoo-do
judo

le ski
lur skee
skiing

l'escalade
less-ka-lad
rock climbing

ON THE TOWN

C'est ma maison.
Say ma may-zon.
This is my house.

J'habite un immeuble.
Sha-beet urn eem-ur-bl.
I live in a block of flats.

un zoo
urn zo
a zoo

un cybercafé
urn see-bair ka-fay
an Internet café

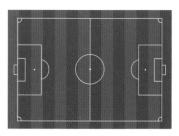

un terrain de foot
urn terr-an dur foot
a football pitch

un centre sportif
urn saun-tr spor-teef
a sports centre

une piscine
oon pee-seen
a swimming pool

une bibliothèque
oon bib-lee-o-tek
a library

un hôtel
urn no-tel
a hotel

un restaurant
urn rest-o-raun
a restaurant

un salon de coiffure
urn sal-on dur kwa-foor
a hairdresser's salon

Il y a un café près d'ici?
Eel ee a urn ka-fay pray dee-see?
Is there a coffee shop near here?

Le parc d'attractions, c'est génial!
Lur park da-traks-yon, say shay-nee-al!
The theme park is brilliant!

un commissariat de police
urn kom-iss-ar-ya
dur pol-eess
a police station

un musée
urn moo-zay
a museum

une poste
oon posst
a post office

un jardin public
urn shar-dan poo-bleek
a park

un cinéma
urn see-nay-ma
a cinema

un camping
urn kaun-ping
a campsite

des toilettes
day twa-let
toilets

un office du tourisme
urn no-feess doo too-ree-sm
a tourist information office

un hôpital
urn nop-ee-tal
a hospital

SHOP TILL YOU DROP

J'adore faire du shopping avec mes copains!
Sha-dor fair doo shop-ping av-ek may kop-an!
I love shopping with my friends!

Ça coûte combien?
Sa koot kom-bee-an?
How much does this cost?

Vingt euros, s'il vous plaît.
Van ur-o, seel voo play.
Twenty euros, please.

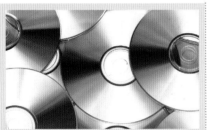

un magasin de musique
urn ma-ga-zan dur moo-zeek
a music shop

un magasin de jeux
urn ma-ga-zan dur shur
a game store

un magasin de vêtements
urn ma-ga-zan dur vet-maun
a clothes shop

un magasin de souvenirs
urn ma-ga-zan dur soo-vur-neer
a gift shop

un magasin de sports
urn ma-ga-zan dur spor
a sports shop

une pâtisserie
oon pat-ee-sur-ee
a cake shop

un magasin de chaussures
urn ma-ga-zan dur sho-soor
a shoe shop

un supermarché
urn soo-pair-mar-shay
a supermarket

Je voudrais deux cartes postales,
s'il vous plaît.
Sh voo-dray dur kart poss-tal, seel voo play.
I'd like two postcards, please.

Ah non! C'est trop cher!
Ar non, say tro shair!
Oh no! It's too expensive!

un CD
urn say-day
a CD

des timbres
day tan-br
stamps

un parapluie
urn pa-ra-plwee
an umbrella

des piles
day peel
batteries

des bonbons
day bon-bon
sweets

un gloss
urn gloss
lip gloss

un magazine
urn ma-ga-zeen
a magazine

du parfum
doo parf-an
perfume

ouvert
oo-vair
open

fermé
fair-may
closed

ENTREE

entrée
aun-tray
entrance

sortie
sor-tee
exit

SCHOOL DAZE

Je suis super bon en maths.
Sh swee soo-per bon aun mat.
I'm very good at maths.

Je suis nulle en arts plastiques.
Sh swee nool aun nar plass-teek.
I'm terrible at art.

J'ai beaucoup de devoirs!
Shay bo-koo dur duv-waar!
I have a lot of homework!

Je vais à l'école à pied.
Sh vay a lay-kol a pee-yay.
I walk to school.

Moi, j'y vais en bus.
Mwa, shee vay aun booss.
I take the bus.

Les matières scolaires
Lay mat-ee-air scol-air
School subjects

le français
le fraun-say
French

l'espagnol
lesp-an-yol
Spanish

la géographie
la shay-o-gra-fee
Geography

l'histoire
lis-twaar
History

les sciences
lay see-aunss
Science

l'informatique
lan-for-ma-teek
I.C.T.

l'art dramatique
lar dra-ma-teek
Drama

la technologie
la tek-no-lo-shee
Technology

l'EPS
lur-pay-ess
P.E.

Dans la classe
Daun la klass
Inside the classroom

le prof
lur prof
teacher

un tableau
urn ta-blo
a board

les élèves
lay zay-lev
students

un bureau
urn boo-ro
a desk

une chaise
oon shez
a chair

Les cours commencent à 8 h 45.
Lay koor ko-maunss a weet ur ka-raunt-sank.
School starts at 8:45.

Les cours finissent à 15 h 30.
Lay koor fee-neess a kanz ur traunt.
School finishes at 3:30.

Dans mon cartable
Daun mon car-ta-bl
In my school bag

des stylos
day stee-lo
pens

des crayons
day kray-yon
pencils

une trousse
oon trooss
a pencil case

une gomme
oon gom
an eraser

un cahier
urn ka-yay
an exercise book

une clé USB
oon klay oo-ess-bay
a memory stick

un dictionnaire
urn dik-see-on-nair
a dictionary

une calculatrice
oon kal-coo-la-treess
a calculator

OUT AND ABOUT

D'habitude, on prend le bus
pour aller en ville.
*Dab-it-ood, on praun lur booss poor
al-lay aun veel.*
We usually get the bus to go to town.

Deux allers simples pour Granville,
s'il vous plaît.
*Dur zal-lay san-pl poor graun-veel,
seel voo play.*
Two singles to Granville, please.

un avion
urn nav-yon
a plane

un bateau
urn bat-o
a boat/ferry

une moto
oon mo-to
a motorbike

un taxi
urn tak-see
a taxi

un aéroport
urn na-ero-por
an airport

un train
urn tran
a train

une voiture
oon vwa-toor
a car

un (auto)bus
urn (ot-o) booss
a bus

un scooter
urn skoo-tair
a scooter

un arrêt de bus
urn nar-ay dur booss
a bus stop

une gare
oon gar
a railway station

Pour aller à la gare, s'il vous plaît?
Poor al-lay a la gar, seel voo play?
Can you tell me how to get to the station, please?

Continuez cette rue.
Kon-tin-oo-ay set roo.
Carry on down this road.

Le prochain train pour... est à quelle heure?
Lur prosh-an tran poor... et a kel ur?
What time is the next train to...?

C'est quel quai?
Say kel kay?
Which platform is it?

Tournez à droite.
Toor-nay a drwat.
Turn right.

Tournez à gauche.
Toor-nay a gosh.
Turn left.

Allez tout droit.
Al-lay too drwa.
Go straight on.

au rond-point
o ron-pwan
at the roundabout

au carrefour
o kar-foor
at the crossroads

aux feux
o fur
at the traffic lights

au pont
o pon
at the bridge

Pour aller à la plage, s'il vous plaît?
Poor al-lay a la plash, seel voo play?
How do I get to the beach?

Prenez le 23.
Pren-ay lur van trwa.
Take bus 23.

JUST THE JOB

Je voudrais être docteur.
Sh voo-dray et-tr dok-tur.
I'd like to be a doctor.

un sportif ♂/une sportive ♀
urn spor-teef/oon spor-teev
a sportsperson

un ♂/une ♀ dentiste
urn/oon daun-teest
a dentist

un ♂/une ♀ vétérinaire
urn/oon vet-ay-ree-nair
a vet

un ♂/une ♀ journaliste
urn/oon shoor-na-lee-st
a journalist

Après le lycée, je vais
travailler dans un magasin.
*A-pray lur lee-say, sh vay tra-va-yay
daun zurn ma-ga-zan.*
When I leave school, I'm going to
work in a shop.

un bureau
urn boo-ro
an office

en plein air
aun plen-air
outdoors

une usine
oon oo-zeen
a factory

un chef
urn shef
a chef

un mécanicien ♂/une mécanicienne ♀
urn may-ka-nee-see-an /oon may-ka-nee-see-en
a mechanic

un ♂/une ♀ photographe
urn/oon fo-to-graf
a photographer

un pompier
urn pomp-yay
a firefighter

un ♂/une ♀ scientifique
urn/oon see-aun-tee-feek
a scientist

un agent de police
urn a-shaun dur po-leess
a police officer

J'ai un petit boulot.
Shay urn pur-tee boo-lo.
I have a part-time job.

Je fais du baby-sitting.
Sh fay doo bay-bee-sit-ting.
I do babysitting.

Je livre les journaux le matin.
Sh lee-vr lay shoor-no lur ma-tan.
I deliver newspapers in the morning.

Je sors des chiens.
Sh sor day shee-an.
I walk dogs.

Je tonds la pelouse.
Sh ton la pe-looz.
I mow the lawn.

FEELING GOOD?

Comment ça va?
Kom-aun sa va?
How are you?

 Pas terrible.
Pa tay-ree-bl.
Not so great.

 Ça va bien, merci.
Sa va bee-an, mer-see.
I'm fine, thanks.

Je suis content ♂/contente.♀
Sh swoe kon-taun/kon-taunt.
I'm happy.

Je suis triste.
Sh swee treest.
I'm sad.

J'ai peur.
Shay pur.
I'm scared.

Je m'ennuie un peu.
Sh maun-nwee urn pur.
I'm a bit bored.

Je m'amuse bien ici.
Sh ma-mooz bee-an ee-see.
I'm having fun here.

Je suis en colère.
Sh swee aun ko-lair.
I'm angry.

Qu'est-ce que tu en penses?
Kes-ka too aun paunss?
What do you think?

C'est vraiment cool!
Say vray-maun kool!
It's really cool!

génial
shay-nee-al
great

nul
nool
rubbish

facile
fa-seel
easy

amusant
a-moo-zaun
fun

difficile
dee-fee-seel
difficult

intéressant
an-tay-ress-aun
interesting

Ça ne va pas?
Sa nur va pa?
Not feeling well?

J'ai mal aux dents.
Shay mal o daun.
I have toothache.

J'ai faim.
Shay fan.
I'm hungry.

J'ai soif.
Shay swaff.
I'm thirsty.

J'ai envie de vomir.
Shay aun-vee dur vo-meer.
I feel sick.

J'ai froid.
Shay frwa.
I'm cold.

J'ai de la fièvre.
Shay dur la fee-ay-vr.
I've got a temperature.

Je voudrais voir un docteur.
Sh voo-dray vwaar urn dok-tur.
I'd like to see a doctor.

J'ai chaud.
Shay sho.
I'm hot.

Je suis fatigué♂/
fatiguée.♀
Sh swee fa-tee-gay.
I'm tired.

J'ai sommeil.
Shay so-may-ee.
I feel sleepy.

J'ai mal au ventre.
Shay mal o vaun-tr.
I've got a stomach ache.

J'ai mal à la tête.
Shay mal a la tet.
I've got a headache.

PRONUNCIATION GUIDE

French	How to make this sound
a	'a' as in 'cat'
e/eu	'ur' as in 'blur'
i	'ee' as in 'machine' (but shorter)
o/au/eau	'o' as in 'mole'
u/ou	'oo' as in 'moon'
ai/ei/è/ê/ë/é/e/er	'ay' as in 'hay'
oi	'wa' as in 'wagon'
ui	'wee' as in 'week'
eil	ay–ee
an/en	'aun' as in 'aunt' (through the nose)
on	'on' as in 'bond' (through the nose)
in/ain	'an' as in 'bang' (through the nose)
un	'urn' as in 'burn' (through the nose)
c	'c' as in 'cat' or 's' as in 'sit'
ç	'ss' as in 'hiss'
ch	'sh' as in 'shell' (not tch)
g	'g' as in gum or 'sh' as in 'treasure'
h	is not pronounced
j	'sh' as in 'treasure' (not dj)
gn	'ny' as in 'canyon'
qu	'k' as in 'kit'
r	roll at the back of the throat
th	't' as in 'Thomas'
w	'v' as in 'van'

* In English you often stress part of the word. However in French you don't do this:

English: crocodile
CRO-co-dile
(X-x-x)

French: crocodile
kro-ko-deel
(x-x-x)

b, d, f, k, l, m, n, p, s, t, v, x, y, z   as in English

* In French you can make a statement into a question by making your voice go up at the end:

Statement: C'est bon.   Question: C'est bon?
Say bon.   *Say bon?*
It's good.   Is it good?